Confessions of a FAITHFUL SLACKER

7 Steps to Renewing Your Relationship with Christ

LISA YVETTE PEARSON

ISBN 978-0-9827-3873-3

Library of Congress Control Number: 2015908569

FHG Unlimited, LLC
237 Flatbush Avenue, #169
Brooklyn, NY 11217

Printed in the United States of America

Love Notes

The purpose of this book is to help us to see ourselves as we are (based on our actions,) discover how we sometimes block ourselves from seeing His face, and the importance of giving our hearts to God in order to restore and renew our individual relationships with God.

ACKNOWLEDGMENTS

Thank You Father for the sacrifice of Your Son Jesus Christ! Thank You for choosing me to be a vessel for Your good works. Your love has given me the strength and courage needed to be who You intended me to be.

For my Pastor Dr. A.R. Bernard... You have helped to shape my spiritual life and guide me on my journey with your teachings. You are, indeed, amazing. Thank you.

For my grandmother Elaine...You did His work by loving us, teaching us, and praying for and with us. I am blessed to have had you in my corner. RIP My Love.

For Mommy and Daddy ...Thank you is not big enough. I love you forever ever.

For my sisters and my bro. Thanks for being my biggest supporters and haters at the same time. I'd have it no other way. I love yall.

For my three little bears. You make Auntie better. I love you always.

For my Sisters and Brothers in Christ who allowed me into their worlds to make this book great: thank you.

For my contributors, sponsors, and donors who helped birth this baby: N. Ellis, Diamond McNulty, Shonte Press, E. Ellis, Carleen Jamison, Monica Mitchell, Deborah Mitchell, Newton Paul, Kyle Poinsette, Jolene Joseph | Alcira Charles, Camille Exil, Clifford Exil, Carmela Gobern, Janna King, Nyree McCray, Malaika

Mears, Sabrina Mompoint, Akwasi Prempeh, Elaine Thompson, Donna Williams, Jorge Zapata, Sharon Alston, Alana Pearson, Nicole McCray, Alcira Boxill, Hardene Etienne, Jason Lowe, M. Pearson, L. Pearson, Diana Wint | J. Arlain, Duane Bryant

For my 90 Day Success Challenge Group…We did it!

For Dee Marshall and Girlfriends Pray…Your ministry has added onto my spiritual journey in ways that are priceless. Thank you.

For Srs. Paulette, Pat, and Lynn…thank you for laying the foundation of faith and education.

For Mrs. Wilken…Thank you for the English blueprint.

For Elaine Thompson…When I was having trouble with completing a project, you said pray to God as the Omega – the Finisher of our faith. He is that and more. And here we are…

For my editor Cristina Veran…The grammar gods are well pleased. Thank you.

For Gail Harry, Lavell Finerson, and Keith L. Forest…thank you for helping me get His vision out.

For Christian Cultural Center, Greater Allen Cathedral A.M.E., and Greater Trinity Baptist Church…Thank you.

Faith-ful
Adjective
    1.   loyal, constant, and steadfast
Synonyms: loyal, constant, true, devoted, unswerving, staunch, steadfast, dedicated, committed
    2.   Having a strong belief in a particular religion
    3.   True to the acts or the original
Synonyms: accurate, precise, exact, errorless, unerring, faultless, true, close, strict

Slack-er* \'sla-ker\
Noun 1898
    1.   A person who shirks work or obligation
    2.   A person and especially a young person who is perceived to be disaffected, apathetic, cynical, or lacking ambition
    3.   An underachiever

*This is also a word often associated with procrastination and mediocrity.

Contents

PRAYER RESOURCES

The Confession

Forgive me Father, for I have sinned.

I've turned my back on You more times than I can count; choosing the plans I made for myself over the plans You've had for me. I've chosen my will over Yours, and my own foolish pride over Your glory. I've made excuses for my sins and rationalized my behavior by using the world as my marker, rather than living by and trusting in Your Word. I've been lukewarm and lazy in my approach to You; doing just enough to feel like I had a relationship with You. But I want the real thing.

So today I choose excellence. I choose to submit to the Holy Spirit, put You first in my life, and to pursue this relationship with You with all my heart. I thank You in advance for Your forgiveness and the new mercies that You grant each and every single day.

I love you. And I thank You for loving me.
In Jesus' Name,
Amen.

The Truth

Even after I turned my life over to Christ, I was still not truly living for God. When I kept feeling a certain emptiness made so by the Holy Spirit knocking on the doors of my heart, I realized how far I was from living for God. That prayer and its many variations became key to the healing and restoration of my heart and my relationship with Him. With the help of some of my sisters and brothers in Christ, I will tell you how you can to get to the healing. But first, let me tell you a little bit about my personal journey.

The Introduction

I came into this world on a hot summer August morning, forty-five days before my expected arrival into this world. I weighed only 4lbs. 6 oz. and my liver was underdeveloped. My parents were simultaneously overjoyed and overwhelmed, to say the least. Twenty-two days after that, I was released from the hospital. Seven days following my release, my mother had me baptized in the Roman Catholic Church. Before I had all my immunization shots, I had Jesus.

As a child, I always knew God was real. Not because I went to Catholic school for eight years, or because my grandmother went to church two to three times a week, twice on Sunday, with prayer meetings, church retreats and church breakfasts sprinkled in. That wasn't it at all. Those things may have laid the foundation, but in my heart, His presence was real.

Still, going to church was either something I *had* to do, or something I would do only because my friends were going. It was not something I actually *wanted* to do. Other than that, I didn't see the point. I didn't feel a personal connection to Jesus. I mean, who was He? Did he have a sense of humor? What did He like? Football? Potato chips? Yes, He performed miracles and healed the sick, but He was too abstract.

I'd learned about Jesus just as though He were part of my school's curriculum, like English and Math. I knew the things I learned in those classes (about prepositional phrases, trigonometry and, yes, Jesus) would help me somewhere down the road. I just didn't know how.

And so, I went about my life with Jesus in the shadows, never really seeking Him except (when I remembered) to say my prayers at night.

Many, many years later, after graduating from junior college, I began going back to church. There was no catalyst (other than God) to send me there; no friends in the back rows like when I was a teenager, and no broken heart in search of comfort.

I just knew I wanted to go. Again, there was no connection to Him.

Except...

One Sunday at Mass, the lector gave a reading about the parable of the talents (Matthew 25:14-30). Though talents were actually a form of currency, because the verse is a parable it made sense to apply the term "talents" to the skills and abilities that we possess. This was groundbreaking for me because I'd been wandering; not really sure of what I would do with my life. Then suddenly, I learn that God gave us "talents" that we were to use or lose. In hindsight, I realized that, since everything we have comes from God, nothing - not talents, not love nor money - is ours to keep. Rather, it must all be shared and, in doing so, will thus be multiplied. I went home and opened up my Bible.

Miracles

I loved my grandmother's faith. She trusted God for every single thing. Once, when I was looking for a job, she told me to pray to a particular saint (I don't remember which one) and ask for help. I asked her why I couldn't just pray "directly to the Source," and she replied, "Sometimes, you need a lawyer!" I did as she advised, and guess what! I got a job shortly after! Still, something was missing. Yes, God could answer our prayers, but that, to me, felt like going to the bank: All transaction, no relationship. Where was God? Would He speak to me? Would I hear Him? I knew He was real, but I needed to hear from Him and get to know Him.

God Speaks

Shortly after I got that new job, I found the answers I had been looking for. At the time, I was dating a handsome older man who worked with me. One day, he asked if I went to church. I told him I did, but that I didn't really connect while there. Instead, I'd be daydreaming about food, what I'd wear the next day, and even have vivid flashbacks of sex. (Yes, I was unmarried and fornicating. Yes, I was thinking about fornicating some more.)

When I asked him if he went to church, his answer blew me away! He said something like, "*Amazing... Pastor ...dynamic ...apply the Word to your life* ..." Whoa! I'd never heard anyone, anywhere, at any time describe their church experience with this much passion! I felt it, too! I said to him, "Maybe I could go with you one day..." which was, surprisingly, followed by silence. You could hear a cotton ball hit the floor. Apparently, that wasn't a good idea because his daughter's mother also went to that same church.
So how did I respond? I did what any other young lady would do if she were in my shoes: I marched into that church, after waiting on a two-hour line, the following Sunday. I was searching for Jesus.

And trouble. Don't judge me.

I didn't see him or her. God knows what He's doing. The "Pastor" was indeed amazing. People were listening intently and taking notes, like they were in class. The Word of God was alive, and it made sense in my life! It spoke to me. *God* had spoken to me. On my next visit (despite the two-hour wait and minus the boyfriend) I went down to the altar and turned my life over to Christ.

That guy and I didn't make it, but I am forever thankful that we crossed paths. He shared His relationship with Christ, and via the Holy Spirit, led me to the exact thing I was searching for: a relationship.

Saved and Sinning...

I wish I could say that after I went down to the altar, the very next day I was the picture of Christianity; loving, evangelizing, living a sin-free life. But I wasn't. I didn't get wings or a halo, either. In fact, the temptation to sin seemed greater. But every decision to sin from this day forward became something that caused anguish in my heart. Am I disappointing God? Will He be angry? Would He forgive me? I would work my way out of a lot of sinful situations (1 Corinthians 10:13,) some easier than others. Sometimes, the pressure to do right (when wrong was so much easier and much more fun) became overwhelming and I just pushed Him out of the equation to do what I felt. There I was, searching for and actually finding God, only to turn away from Him.

He was never totally out of the equation, of course. He may have tuned out some of my ridiculous prayers, but He never ever left me. I knew this when the car I was riding in skidded across four lanes of traffic on the busy Belt Parkway on a rainy Saturday afternoon, and neither it, nor any of us inside, had even a scratch. I knew because when my grandmother passed away, though I was sad (because I'd miss her,) I felt peace in my heart. I knew she knew the Lord and had gone home to be with Him. I knew because, even when I was in the midst of my many sins and according to my doctor *thisclose* to dying from food poisoning and dehydration, He sent an angel in the form of a Christian co-worker who saved my life with a simple act of kindness: packing water, ginger ale and crackers into my tote bag before I went home. The only two places I went, once I got home, were my bedroom and the bathroom. I didn't have the strength to go anywhere else. According to my doctor, had I not drunk that water and ginger ale, I

would have become dehydrated, my kidneys could have shut down, and my heart could have stopped.

Even after all that, I still messed up – because we are built that way – and after each time, I would come back to Him, tearful and asking forgiveness. When I felt hurt and empty, because temporary things like drinking and unfulfilling relationships no longer filled the void of His absence, I would turn to Him and the peace would return. He had my back. There would be consequences, but they would be nothing compared to the knowledge that I was back on the right side — on God's side — of things.

Though there were still more years to follow, of willfully bending the rules to do foolishness, finally, I realized that my lukewarm behavior – namely my resistance to doing what I knew was the right thing, while "sort of" praying, obeying, or attending church was pushing me further away from Him. The Bible says, *"I know your deeds, that you are neither cold nor hot. I wish you were either one or the other! So because you are lukewarm – neither hot nor cold, I am about to spit you out of my mouth."* (Rev 3:16)

Aha.

Have you ever had lukewarm coffee or lukewarm tea? It's pretty purposeless to drink, right? It doesn't warm the bones and it doesn't enhance the taste of the coffee beans or the aroma of the tea leaves. It's just "blah." That's the direction I truly felt that I was heading in: spit out of God's mouth. The lessons I had to learn were repeating themselves and getting harder because I wasn't listening—and the fallouts after each lesson were getting worse. I would hear a directive from God and do the direct opposite. For that, I suffered.

Why, you may ask, if God instructed me to do something, would I choose to do the exact opposite? The answer to that question is that I thought I could still have it my way. I had to learn that life with God is not like ordering at Burger King – where I can have it my way. It is His will be done, not mine.

Building and Rebuilding the Relationship

In the beginning, God was more of an acquaintance than anything, like the co-worker we might only talk to at work (or that church friend with whom we only chat on Sundays,) then go our separate ways. But when I began to submit my heart to Him, to really seek Him, to know Him better and learn to trust Him and love Him and believe Him, the relationship grew stronger.

On those days when I would shut Him out, I would feel distant and alone (and guilty, at times,) because I knew I had turned my back. The separation and the distance from God was purely from my end, of course. Sometimes, it came from disappointment, because I asked God to do something but it didn't happen. Mostly though, the distance was brought on by my impatience, which led to sin.

How does one lead to the other? Just a few years ago, as my faith had been growing stronger, deepening my relationship with God, I came to know that abstaining before marriage would be an important part of my Christian walk. Then I met a man.

He was not only a Christian, he was handsome, smart and tall. I was attracted to him, and despite those aforementioned convictions, I wanted a physical relationship with him.

Then one day, in prayer, I heard from God. He said that this man was "not my husband." In that moment, my eyes flew open and I looked around the room, to see if someone else was there. But no, it was just me, the sofa and the four walls—and God. (Note: Y'all. I was sad. I thought I'd found my Boaz!) I liked that man though, and stubbornly moved forward, despite knowing I wasn't supposed to. I was impatient to have what I wanted, when I wanted it. The sin was two-fold. Not only did I sin with my body, but I sinned in my disobedience. Waiting for God took too long, I felt, and so I took matters into my own hands—but this did not get the results I expected. Instead of letting God work on me, to set me up for His greater plans, I got in the way with my own plans and immature needs. This cost me time and lots of pain.

The God of Second (Third, Fourth, and Fifth) Chances

I second-guessed God many times, sometimes to the point of disobedience. But those painful days and nights of living with rejection, depression, and the guilt of disappointing God taught me to listen to, and for, His voice – and to be obedient.

You are reading a book that He inspired back on January 1, 2010 during prayer. It took a lot of time to put His plan into effect though, because I just wasn't ready to act on it. My relationship with Him still needed strengthening. I needed to mature, to gain a greater understanding of myself and others, in order to grow. During this grooming process, God taught me the value of service. He taught me to how to keep commitments. He even sent people who helped me to honor my commitment to attend church on a regular basis, rather than the sporadic pattern that emulated other areas of my life – like getting to work (or anywhere else) on time, and completing projects I'd started as well. He encouraged me by giving me the courage to take on this task, and the discipline to listen to the needs of others, and for the sound of His voice. I submitted to the call of the Holy Spirit on my life, and to Him, and He performed CPR on me, transforming our relationship forever.

I realized, through all these trials, that although I was indeed a believer I was still trying to let my flesh lead. I was lukewarm in my belief; I did just enough to *feel like* I had a relationship with God, never really letting Him heal me of the brokenness [of abuse, depression, previous hardships, sin, of not feeling like I was enough, and the rest of life's perceived failures.] I'd never surrendered my heart. I'd never really let Him help me, or use me for His glory. It was all about me. *I was a faithful slacker, devoted to mediocrity in my actions towards God;* wanting to put forth minimum work while still expecting maximum results.

Trigonometry has helped me to get a few home improvement projects done, while knowing about prepositions, along with other English grammar terms, have become crucial to my life as a writer. But my need for Jesus far beyond any of those things, is like the need for air.

In writing this book, I was able to strengthen my relationship with Christ in four significant ways.

1. *I learned to listen and be obedient.*
2. *I witnessed His grace and power.*
3. *I learned patience.*
4. *I learned that I couldn't change on my own; that surrender to Jesus was required.*

Although my name is on the cover of this book, as its author, ultimately it is a work of God. He has used me as a vessel to encourage those of you who may not be feeling as close to Him as you might wish to be; Or who may not be feeling comfortable in your church home; Or who are disappointed with the direction in which your life has gone; Or who believed in Him for something that did not come to be; Or who have fallen away because of sin and feel unsure that He'd take you back.

There is so much more I myself need to learn, and I hope that you, too, see God's great grace and mercy in your lives. I pray that deliverance meets you where your desire to sin overwhelms you – where you feel tempted or feel lost - and that You know, without any doubt, how much He loves you.

God, unlike His children, is ever faithful. He promised He would never leave or forsake us. Even after we fail him, He takes us back. If we mess up again, in fact, He'll still be there. All we have to do is turn back in His direction. He is our Father. He wants a relationship with us, His children.

Scripture Meditation

"But when the kindness and love of God our Savior appeared, he saved us, not because of righteous things we have done, but because of His mercy. He saved us through the washing of rebirth and renewal by the Holy Spirit, whom he poured out on us generously through Jesus Christ our Savior, so that having been justified by grace we might become heirs having the hope of eternal life." (Titus 3:4-7 NIV)

Quiz

If you are not sure if you fall into the *Faithful Slacker* category, here is a short quiz to help figure it out. Mark *X* for the ones that apply to you.

___ My Bible is as clean as Pastor's church suit; with not a speck of dirt, a crease, or an occasional pen mark. It's also my drink coaster, bookend and decoration on my nightstand.

___ When I leave church on Sunday, the next time I talk to God is the following Sunday. That's His day, isn't it?

___ Tithing is putting just two dollars in the collection plate, even though I bring in a healthy salary.

___ I don't need to go to church to believe in God.

___ I say "you're lucky I'm saved" at least three times a week. Usually *after* I've behaved like a donkey in front of an audience. Hey, I'm only human. And God knows my heart.

___ Habakkuk? What in the world is a Habakkuk? And how do you pronounce that?

___ I don't feel close to God, because He hasn't answered my prayers.

If you marked an *X* on this quiz, read on faithful slacker.

Journal Starters

Use your journal entry as a starting point to getting to the bottom of the distance you are/were experiencing in your relationship. Open with a simple prayer of thanksgiving for His presence. Ask the Holy Spirit to guide you. There is no right or wrong answer, experience, or feeling. Here are a few prompts to get you started.

1. My earliest memory of God was...

2. I made a decision to pursue God when I...

3. The time(s) I felt furthest from God was when...

4. The time(s) I felt closest to God was when...

5. When I feel distant from God, I believe that God...

THE FAITHFULLY UNFAITHFUL SLACKER

If you see yourself in any of these profiles and you feel angry or convicted, it's the Holy Spirit at work in your heart. It was not until I saw the real me - showcased in some of these profiles - that I could accept myself as imperfect, understand God's perfect love, and allow the Holy Spirit to work on me, in me, and through me.

The Homebodies

Mr. Homebody

This faithful slacker says things like, "I don't need to go to church to believe in God." On Sundays, he is the front row member of Bedside Tabernacle TV Church. He may even tune into his favorite Pastor via Holy Sofa Deliverance Church of the iPad.

Sometimes this slacker turns to "at home services" because he feels burned out; over-churched and tired. It happens!

But other times, he just refuses to drum up the time or energy to actually leave his home. *I have so much to do and, between working two jobs, I'm tired. The seventh day is a day of rest and besides, God knows my heart.* He treats God like an afterthought; a friend that he takes for granted.

This guy probably says things like, *I don't have*

to take my girlfriend out on dates or call her every day to have a good relationship. Then he wonders why she moves on to someone else who willingly invests that time in her!

This homebody may also use excuses like: *I'm tired. It's too cold outside. It's too hot. It's raining.* Or, *I'll just go next week* – a date which never arrives. But let there be a party or an all-you-can-eat buffet... suddenly, this guy is more reliable than the postal service. Rain, sleet, or snow, he is there.

Ms. Homebody

This sister says things like, *Oh, please. The church is filled with hypocrites.* Or she might say, *I don't feel like I belong there.* Sometimes, there really is a matter of her not feeling included, loved or protected in her house of worship. Judgment against her and others may have infiltrated the body of the church and she no longer feels like she belongs there. The love of her brothers and sisters may have gone cold, and revealing herself to others has left her feeling exposed and hurt. Or, disillusionment with a pastor or a church official may have left a sour taste because she comes to realize her Pastor, whom she has idolized is actually a sinner, too.

Homebody Jr.

This slacker not only says, *I don't have to go to church to believe in God.* He or she also (conveniently) wonders, *How do we even know if the Bible is real? 'They' say the Bible is just a bunch of stories made up by men, not God.*

This slacker may feel like he never hears directly from God while another, when she is at church, never feels like the message is directed at her, so she checks out altogether. Then, too, there are those who'd just prefer to receive an instant Word in our instant society; everything packed for instant digital delivery, from the comfort of home, without having to navigate traffic, weather, or other people.

Staying away feels good for many different reasons— or we, as slackers, wouldn't do it.

1) It means we don't have to face the people who've hurt us, or the people we ourselves have let down.

2) It makes us feel like we have some sort of control over our lives, because the rest of the week, between work or school, or family responsibilities, belongs to everyone else. If nothing else, God will understand.

Doubting the contents or authors of the Bible, simply out of "convenience," allows us to maintain an autonomy over our lives where we can:

    a) deny or manipulate God's standards for our lives.

    b) subconsciously have a safety net when things go awry. We don't flat-out say "no, He doesn't exist," because we still want God to hear us when we come to him with our problems. (He will. It's called grace—but we have no control over it.)

Watching services online or on television recognizes and acknowledges (even inadvertently) our need for His word, but the downside to receiving it in this manner is that, according to Dr. A.R. Bernard of Christian Cultural Center in Brooklyn, NY, "We don't grow in isolation. We grow in community."

We grow as people in Christ when we are together.

Rev. Danny Curry of Greater Trinity Baptist Church in Queens, NY, says "You can stay home and pray, but the Bible says that where two or three gather together [touching and agreeing,] the Spirit of God is there, too.* So where the presence of God is, there's strength. When you are there with your brothers and sisters praying, the Spirit of God comes in and makes the change."

So, no, this slacker doesn't *have* to go to church to believe in God, but (1) he or she will have a much better chance of developing a relationship with God and strengthening it while among other believers who, believe it or not, need his prayers just as much. And (2) the people are the church. You and I make up the body of Christ. (1 Cor. 12:27) No people = no church.

Furthermore, going to church is an intentional action that says, *I know You are everywhere, but I want to be in your holy presence in Your house.* Sure, it's good to call your old grandpa on the phone to say you're thinking of him, but it's better yet to drop in for a visit.

Furthermore, going to church is about worship. We go to church to worship. Yes, we ask for things when we are there, peace, comfort, guidance, help (in all things,) but the church experience is about giving praise and exalting God. Worship.

Despite what this slacker might think, it's not always about her or him.

*"For where two or three gather in my name, there I am with them."
(Matthew 18:20)

22

The Disclaimant

I *know some scripture and I even get to church on a regular basis, so what I do that isn't God-like is excused by this "Get Out of Hell Free" disclaimer: God knows my heart.*

Yes, she'll change the tag on the expensive shirt so that she can pay less – which is stealing – but justify it with: God knows my heart. This is a faithful slacker style excuse. Yes, she cursed that woman out. But God knows her heart, she tells herself. Yes, she tithes two dollars, even though she rakes in six figures, wears a mink to church, and drives a Mercedes Benz. But God knows her heart. Yes, she just came out of service, covered with the dew of praise, but refused to yield to a fellow church member in the parking lot or make eye contact after being so stank. But God knows her heart.

Her using this phrase is actually just a copout to avoid doing the right thing. It's in the same category as *God forgive me, but [insert something judgmental or rude]...* and *I'm just going to do this and ask for forgiveness later,* as though God cannot see through the ruse.

> Galatians 6:7 says, "Do not be deceived: God cannot be mocked. A man reaps what he sows."

So if this slacker believes that "God knows my heart" is going to cancel out her sins or ease the consequences of her actions, it isn't.

Also, keep in mind...

> Matthew 15:18-19 says, "But the things that come out of a person's mouth come from the heart and these defile them. For out of the heart come evil thoughts – murder, adultery, sexual immorality, theft, false testimony, slander."

Ahem.

This faithful slacker may want to consider a new catchphrase to absolve herself the next time she sins. There's help for her, though. God is a God of renewal.

> 2 Corinthians 5:17 (NIV) says, "Therefore, if anyone is in Christ, the new creation has come; the old has gone, the new is here."

Until she truly surrenders her heart to God though, she should know this: God does indeed know her heart. And that heart's not looking too good. At all.

The Blind

You might hear this person say, *I don't believe in God anymore. I believe there is good energy and positivity. There's also bad energy and negativity.* Or, they might say, *I believe that what goes around comes back around – and that's it.* Or, *But if there is a God, how come all these bad things keep happening?*

This person is a slacker only in the sense that he gave up on his faith. Usually, this is someone who believed God while praying for a certain outcome that, ultimately, didn't happen. Subsequently, he is disappointed, hurt and feeling ignored by God so, in turn, he no longer sees God moving in his life or no longer believes that He even exists.

He or she may have been abused, or may have suffered a great loss; or they may have been waiting for some kind of breakthrough for a very long time (by human standards.) Or, they may have been sheltered as a child and raised to expect life to be free from adversity; a field of lilies and butterflies with rainbows.

Here is something to ponder about that field, though: Lilies are flowers, flowers attract butterflies, yes. But they also attract bees. Bees sting. Bee stings hurt. Some of us are allergic to bee stings and have terrible reactions. Furthermore, rainbows require that it rain (sometimes unexpectedly) and mean that the field will be soggy, and your brand new sneakers will get dirty in the mud. The sun will eventually come back out, of course; the flowers will glisten before your eyes, you'll see your rainbow, you might see two, but in that moment you may still have a bee sting, cold, damp clothes, dirty sneakers, and ugly hair.

Get it?

God never promised that we wouldn't have problems. If he had, rest assured, we'd all be living in His heavenly paradise. But he didn't say that.

Most everyone we meet in the Bible has some problem or adversity to contend with. For example, Tamar (Gen. 38:6-27) had two husbands (who were brothers, by the way) whom God killed because they were wicked in His eyes. She chose to sleep with Judah her father-in-law if she was to have children since he'd reneged on his duty to marry her off to his third son. Ewww.

> [Author's Note: During these times, it was common for a brother (or two) to stand in for his deceased brother in order to produce heirs. But ewww.]

Noah (Gen. 6:14) had to build an ark for a flood that no one else could foresee. How much ridicule might he have had to endure? Joseph (Gen. 37:5) was despised by his brothers (because of his great gifts) and sold into slavery. Daniel (Dan. 6:16) was in the lion's den. With lions. Who had really large, sharp teeth and claws. Mary (Luke 1:31) was given the enormous responsibility of giving birth to our Lord. Samson (Judges 16:4) fell in love with the wrong woman. Job lost his family, friends and fortune. Sarah (Gen. 17:17; 21:2) had to wait until she was ninety to have a baby. Ninety. Seriously. Yet God was there every single time. Either to encourage, instruct, direct, comfort, protect or, to deliver on His promises. He was present. Why? Because that is what He promised.

> *Deuteronomy 31:6 says, "Be strong and*
> *courageous. Do not be afraid or terrified*
> *because of them, for the LORD your God*
> *goes with you; he will never leave nor*
> *forsake you."*

So not only will he not leave us, or give up on us, he also encourages us!

> Jeremiah 29:11 says, "For I know the plans I
> have for you," declares the LORD, "plans to
> prosper you and not harm you, plans to give
> you hope and a future."

We wrongly assume that God has to bless our plans, but the truth for believers is that God has a plan for us. And we should be encouraged by the knowledge that He has plans for us! Whatever it is we didn't get, but truly wanted, we must understand that God is either preparing us for it at a later date or has greater things in mind for us.

What we have planned is oftentimes different from what God plans for us. Sometimes, for example, we may be praying on the health of a loved one. Yet, despite this, his or her health fails and we have to say what seems to be a premature goodbye. Whenever I hear of a person dying an untimely death, I often wonder: Was that person's work done here? I like to think so, but we can't know for certain.

There are the other areas, too, where we may feel we have not seen God show up in our lives: Was that thing that we asked for meant for God's glory or to fulfill our own selfish desires? Hmmm. Do we truly believe the Lord's prayer when we mumble through the words "Your Kingdom come, Your will be done?" Or do we really mean, "**My** kingdom come, **my** will be done?"

Some things that may happen in our lives will be impossible to understand, but the psalmist says,

> *"Your love, LORD, reaches the heavens, your faithfulness to the skies." (Psalm 36:5)*

It is *because* His love for us is so great that He does not always give us what we ask for; because it might actually hurt us. He takes away certain things and people so that we might learn to function without them and, instead, lean on Him; or because it was their time to go. We can speculate all day on why He does what He does, but the truth is that we will never fully understand "why." God created us, we did not create Him. Does a painting understand why its creator chose the colors he did? Nope. He knew us before we were formed in the womb. (Psalm 139:15-16) We didn't choose Him. He chose us (John 15:16) and, with the Holy Spirit, in due time, made us aware of Him.

No good parent gives a child every single thing he asks for, because this son or daughter will surely grow unappreciative of what he or she has. A child is not always aware of the danger of some of the things he asks for, either. No good parent will ignore a child's bad behavior, because a child will otherwise not understand the concept of consequences.

God is a good parent. God knows what He is doing with us and why. We may not like or appreciate some of the circumstances and the hurts that accompany these life trials, but the God who created us, who knows us, and who chose us is the same God who loves us to the heavens and skies and wants the best for us. If, despite reading and studying the Bible, all we ever understand about God is that He loves us, and that all things work together for the good of those who love Him, then we still know that He is real.

The Finger Pointer

You might hear this slacker say something like, *Look at Sister June over there, talking about folks. The Bible says in Proverbs 21:23 that "Those who guard their mouths and their tongues keep themselves from calamity."* Or, *Hmph. You know that baby was born out of wedlock. The Bible says in Deuteronomy 23:2 that "No one born of a forbidden marriage (or one of illegitimate birth) nor any of their descendants may enter into the assembly of the LORD, not even in the tenth generation."* Hmmm.

Somewhere in between talking about folks-who-are-talking-about-folks and judging someone else's decisions, the "laws" of the Bible became inflexible, for everyone else but her. She makes a show of showing how knowledgeable she is of the Bible because she is a "good Christian."

"Give unto Caesar what belongs to Caesar..." however, applies to everyone else but her. She justifies her shady tax returns by joking that Caesar lived in Rome and the IRS ain't nowhere in the Bible! In addition, she sleeps with her beau because, (although he hasn't even proposed) she tells herself, they're going to be married anyway. Besides, she's only human. Right. The judgment and scrutiny she gives to others goes all the way down to microscopic proportion. But, well, she's special.

> Luke 6:41 says, "Why do you look at a speck of sawdust in your brother's eye and pay no attention to the plank in your own eye? How can you say to your brother, 'Brother, let me take the speck out of your eye, when you yourself fail to see the plank in your own eye? You hypocrite, first take the plank out of your eye, and then you will see clearly to remove the speck from your brother's eye."

This slacker ought to pray to fix herself, first, before she 'helps' to fix others with her advice or admonitions. No one can truly help another person's state of affairs when they can't even see the condition of their own.

Romans 2:1 says. "You, therefore, have no excuse, you who pass judgment on someone else, for at whatever point you judge another, you are condemning yourself, because you who pass judgment do the same things."

It's so easy to see flaws in others, isn't it? Oftentimes, those are the very same things we despise, or are fighting against, within ourselves. Maybe it's best, then, to point out the good in others instead. And then, you know…maybe something good will come of that.

The Truth Teller

J ust as scripture refers to Christ's teachings by saying, *"the truth shall set you free,"* that, too, is the motto this slacker lives by. Without you asking, he will tell you the reason you're broke, that you need to lose weight, the reason why your marriage isn't working, or why you aren't married in the first place.

It's bad enough that it's none of his business, but he insists upon telling you 'the truth' about yourself without any consideration of your feelings. For him, these have no place in the equation at all. Far from setting you free, "the truth" is that his words shall actually hold you back! There are usually only a few outcomes to such unsolicited advice a.k.a "truths": the person on the receiving end tunes the "truth teller" out completely; the person on the receiving end is wounded by this person's version of truth and believes this person's judgment; or the person on the receiving end strikes back. The truth teller may even convince himself that he is justified because, after all, it was his "duty" to tell the truth.

It is fair to say that the truth teller would be hurt if he were to receive even a tiny dose of his own medicine, however. The real truth is that the truth teller needs to be told that Jesus did all things – even correction - in love.

> James 3:17 says, "But the wisdom that comes from heaven is first of all pure; then peace-loving, considerate, submissive, full of mercy and good fruit, impartial and sincere."

A sincere truth teller, as a Christian, should be sensitive to his friend's demeanor, and want his friend to benefit from his love so that he or she might flourish, rather than wither under the weight of words filled with malice.

> 1 Corinthians 13:1 says, "If I speak in the tongues of men and of angels, but do not have love, I am only a resounding gong or a clanging cymbal."

You know what cymbals sound like when loving hands are playing them? Angelic. Harmonious. Calm. Serene. You know what cymbals sound like when played off beat, by rough, inexperienced hands? Noise. Let's not be noise.

The Lucky One

This slacker has been known to announce, *You're lucky I'm saved* at the strangest moments.

Wait. Let's clarify something first: This slacker label is not intended for those people who have submitted to the Spirit and have learned to "reign in the crazy" and announce this as a point of acknowledging anger and the refusal to give in to it. This is not for the ones who have truly surrendered and are allowing God to correct bad behavior.

No.

This is for the lady who goes off half-cocked in the supermarket because the price of bananas has risen two cents. She curses the cashier and everyone within three-hundred feet – cops included – and then suddenly comes to her senses when she remembers that she is saved, Holy Ghost-filled and fire-baptized.

This is the man who finds himself in the crowded parking lot at the mall. It is ridiculously crowded; Christmas Eve crowded. He's circled around and around. Finally, the mom with the baby stroller signals that she is parked just ahead. Thankful to God for putting him in the right place at the right time, he signals so other drivers will know the space is his. Just as mom begins to back out, another car comes slowly from the other direction. Sure enough the other car zips into the space. It's all holy everything 'til somebody steals your parking space! Nothing that's been said to that driver could ever be said before God. And the space thief's flattened tire isn't really that bad. But somehow we're *lucky* he's saved?

For some reason, these Lucky Saints feel the need to announce their "Saved-ness" as though it should earn them some sort of accolade. Or an excuse to downplay bad behavior, like some self-patting-of-the-back, maybe for not committing murder, "only" assault? I don't know. But such an announcement in those circumstances is unnecessary and disrespectful.

Such a lack of self-control can be difficult to curb. It resonates in many sins – in this case, rage. This person goes from warm-cup-of-tea to whistling kettle in a matter of seconds – often finding him or herself in hot water.

> Proverbs 16:32 says, "Better a patient person than a warrior, one with self-control than one who takes a city."

In other words, a person who is not controlled by their emotions and the need to fight is better in God's eyes than the person who submits to moods and tantrums. Soldiers that study an enemy and can plot out a strategy will always fare better than the one who rushes in with his feelings and emotions as his weapon and shield. Both can be manipulated and used against him.

> Galatians 5:22-23 says, "But the fruit of the Spirit is love, joy, peace, forbearance, kindness, goodness, faithfulness, gentleness and self-control. Against such things there is no law."

These lawful attributes are the bright, beautiful, ripe, Spirit-filled fruits that God would love for us to exhibit! Not some dried, shriveled, rotten flesh-led fruit (sin) that leads us further from Him. When we fail to pray for (and practice) self-control, we allow the Devil a chance to get in and show his face

– to get his fifteen minutes of fame. As Christians, our goal is to always give God the glory!

Rather than saying the phrase to flaunt some kind of superiority over others, this slacker ought to modify it to *I'm Lucky I'm Saved.* Yes, we are indeed.

The Imperfectly Imperfect

This slacker says things like, *I'm never going to be perfect, so why try?* He gives up on greatness before even giving it a fair shot! If that is not a slacker, I don't know what is!

None of us will ever measure up to Christ. Ever. Not even on our best day, in our best suit, or best shoes. Not with our kindest words, or our most sincere and personable gestures. We just can't. The Bible tells us that we *all* fall short of the glory of God. Keyword: all. For this slacker, it's just too much to bear.

But the more we pursue Jesus, the closer we will come to being like Him. The more we work on emulating Jesus, the easier it becomes to turn from sin. But it's not easy. There are huge obstacles designed to deter and detour us from the path. For instance: the minute you are working on anger, that annoying co-worker will come over to your desk and spill his coffee. All. Over. Your. Presentation. Just when you are working on abstaining, you'll run into your ex who is smelling really good and looking really fine and it sure has been a long time. As for the forgiveness you've been working on after last Sunday's sermon... watch how your sister shows up unannounced at your family dinner, wearing the shirt you thought you lost at the laundry.

Sure, we would like if we were to never succumb to anger, lust, or unforgiveness. But we have. We do. We will. Sometimes we fail terribly at mastering our best selves. In fact, we can't ever do so 100%. It's Jesus' job to do that – if we allow Him in. But even if we don't, and we find ourselves struggling with sin, that doesn't mean we should just sign our lives over to the Devil because of the fear of not measuring up! No! That is foolish. In case you haven't heard, foolishness is not God's forte.

> Galatians 6:9 says, "Let us not become weary in doing good, for at the proper time we will reap a harvest if we do not give up."

Your hard work will pay off. Your genuine good deeds will help others, and those good deeds will also be done for you, by others – if you don't cave, lose hope, or quit. Sometimes you may not even see the results, but God does. Your good works continue to build up His Kingdom. Your good works allow others to see God working through you. It's like you are employed by God and you're wearing your clean uniform, giving the best customer service that money can't buy.

> Romans 3:23 says, "For all have sinned and fall short of the glory of God..."

Guess what! Only God is perfect. Only Jesus is perfect. Only the Holy Spirit is perfect. Everyone else? Not so much. What that means is that it's time to get over feeling inadequate and, instead, get into the spirit of living for God!

> Romans 3:24 adds: "and all are justified freely by His grace through the redemption that came by Christ Jesus."

Christ died for us, so that even though we sin and fall short, His grace covers us nevertheless.
The God we serve sees all of our flaws and loves us anyway. He loves us so much that He sacrificed His only Son to be humiliated, tortured and murdered, that we would receive the gift of forgiveness and grace, abundant life and salvation.

When we are tempted to turn away from God for fear of not measuring up, it's important to remember that the Devil doesn't operate with forgiveness and grace like God does, but through blame and condemnation, self-doubt and insecurity. People who choose the Devil's path often end up despondent and depressed. Suicide may be considered and even carried out. Why? Because Satan's ultimate goal is to ruin you and secure your place in Hell.

There are really no in-betweens here. This slacker has a serious decision to make, and he can't afford to choose the wrong team.

These are examples not just of the types of people we all encounter along our daily walk, but also examples of ourselves. No matter how sanctified we may believe ourselves to be, we, as Christians, are not and cannot ever be perfect. This goes back to the first book of the Bible. Adam and Eve disobeyed God, and not much has changed since then. We sin. We get reprimanded. And forgiven. Forgiveness exists because God knows that as human beings, we will inevitably go off track and, at the very least, be like the faithful slackers we've just read about.

We stray because we are disappointed, we feel hurt or, perhaps, just plain weary from the walk. The lure of sin is strong. Even when God has us in a place where He is refining us, the Devil has a habit of showing up. Sometimes, we take the old familiar bait; Or sometimes the bait may be shiny new and calling our names. Yet, still, God draws us back in.

It's time to stop fighting His love. Let Him draw you back in.

Journal Starters

Open your journal entry with a prayer inviting the Holy Spirit in. Be still and ask the Holy Spirit to reveal to you the things that may be hindering your relationship. Use your journal as a starting point. There is no right or wrong answer, experience, or feeling. Here are a few prompts to get you started.

1. The things I do that block others from seeing His light within me include…

2. I know I cannot or will ever be perfect, but today I will ask Him to help me work on…

3. The things I need Him to help me overcome most are…

4. The one thing I need prayer and intervention with are…

7 WAYS TO RENEW YOUR RELATIONSHIP WITH CHRIST

A House is Not a Home

1.

Find a church home that fits you best.

What makes a house a *home* is not the building itself, but the people inside who share common experiences with us. It's the people who we grow with, even through discomfort. A home is where we normally find our peace.

To rightly be called Christians means that we accept Jesus Christ as our Lord and Savior. We believe that he died for our sins. To be saved means that we have surrendered our lives to Christ and want to live by His standard.

Whether we do or not succeed in this journey depends on the choices we make. One that can determine whether or not we will be sufficiently armed to truly live by His standard is the church home where we decide to worship.

There are many kinds of churches to choose from, separated by denomination, factions and/or size. Some congregations jump and shout, while some are more reserved. Some churches preach brimstone and fire, while others emphasize forgiveness and redemption. Some churches are small, cozy, familial affairs where, if you're new, you may either enjoy this level of closeness or otherwise feel excluded. Some are huge in size, leaving a newcomer to either feel like a kernel in a cornfield or embracing a little anonymity that might enable someone to ease-in at his or her own pace.

There are many different ways to praise the Lord. All believe in Christ. All have different practices and offer different environments in which to worship. This is why choosing and committing to just one is a delicate and sensitive process; one we may unwittingly nullify by choosing a congregation for convenience and familiarity over the direction of the Holy Spirit and the church's potential to foster our spiritual growth and fulfillment.

What exactly is spiritual growth? The process begins in our being born an infant in Christ, drinking only milk, continuing through until we become mature enough for solid food. *(1Corinthians 3:2)* It is the way your relationship with God matures and seeps into other areas of your life – trusting Him through all things and for all things. It's how we learn to pray with conviction and rely on the power of God.

For that person who declares that they do not have to actually go to church to believe in God, Rev. Danny Curry cautions, "The church building is just an object. So while it's true we don't have to go to church to believe in God, it is also true that it is the people within the building (including you) who make up the church."

For the homebody who feels abandoned or the person whose spirit just cannot embrace the word of God in a particular setting, sometimes a change of scenery is the remedy.

The Perfect Fit

Finding a church is like finding the perfect pair of jeans or the perfect power tool. Youthful wisdom buys the latest style or model, whether or not the fit is a good one. Perhaps, because your friends are wearing the same style, or because it's pretty hard to find something you really like (and can afford) you just get what you can. In the case of jeans, this can lead to exposed undergarments, a muffin top, or split seams. With regard to power tools, the wrong choice could result in a messy home improvement project or a trip to the emergency room.

Not all styles fit properly, however, so we should look for the jeans that enhance our positives; the ones that have some stretch that allows us to grow. The right power tool, meanwhile, should come with a weight and speed you can handle, good instructions and the number to the help desk.

Finding the right church is a similar task. If you are not being fed where you are, first pray for His guidance and then ask around. There will surely be somewhere to draw you in.

Hardene E. recalls how, after a move out of state, she had to find a new church home. When going into any church house, she explains "I pray about it: 'Lord, lead me to where you want me to be, where I can be used for your glory. Bless me to be able to eat the meat and spit out the bones, and not be so concerned about anything but your word'."

Nisla E. shares that although her mom "always forced" her family to go to church, it was "the youth programs, the retreats, leader and mentee programs, the youth choir" that kept her going back. "The youth program helped set a foundation for me," she remembers. "I was there from [age] thirteen to about seventeen, eighteen when I left to go to school." Upon her return from school (and few ups and downs) she returned to her church and is now a part of its ministry program.

Minister Cee says that before he found Christ, he was "definitively an agnostic," though "in deep search," and "bouncing between churches." He'd visited his present church home because of an invitation in 1996, but despite the Word, he could not accept waiting in line for two hours to attend the services that were filled to capacity. When he, one day, diffused an altercation on the subway however, he heard God say, "You'll never be able to reach anyone if you don't go back." He became a member of his current congregation in 1997, where he serves in a ministerial and leadership capacity.

The Holy Spirit will lead you to where you are supposed to be by opening your heart to receive this direction or revelation. Sometimes God uses another vessel through whom to invite you. Maybe, for example, you might visit a church because the music of its choir comforts you and speaks to your soul, always seeming to open your heart to His presence. God knows who we are and He knows exactly what bait he needs to reel us in. Wherever it is He ultimately leads you, you can trust that the fit will be in alignment with your needs and His plan for you.

Journal Starters

Open your journal entry with a simple prayer for guidance. Be still and ask the Holy Spirit to lead you to the right place of worship. Use your journal as a starting point to list any misgivings you have about church (yours or church in general.) Use your journal to list a few churches you have been meaning to visit. Here are a few prompts to get you started.

1. The last time I went to church, I had issues with...

2. The things I enjoy about going to church are...

3. The one church that I've been meaning to visit is...

4. The three things I need from a church home are...

That's What Friends Are For

2.

Talk to trusted, rational—and saved—friends.

Not all of your friends who profess to be saved can be trusted with guiding your spiritual life, however. Not all (including saved) friends are rational.

We are all at different stages from one another in our relationships with God. If you're feeling distance from Him, you may want to talk to a more mature person; someone who may have been through a similar season, as opposed to someone just getting acclimated, who has either not experienced what you are going through, or, may have dealt with it in a way that was not truly Spirit-led.

Everyone's walk with God is different, and so we have to know where we should best turn for guidance. We ought to steer clear of those who are fanatical, seeking a glorification of themselves rather than God.

It is surely important that the person be balanced, thoughtful and interested in your growth as a Christian. They should be encouraging and patient. They should be willing to listen and willing to explain things from a spiritual perspective, as well as, a worldly perspective.

A minister or priest is ideal, but if neither is an option, look for that person at work who you know is a believer. Or a family member who is. Or even that friend nicknamed "The Church Lady" in your phone. They are around for a reason. You will know if they are trustworthy by how they speak and carry themselves, whether or not they admit to sin and imperfection. If they don't admit to their own state of sin, instead pretending that they are perfect at all times, ask them to see the holes from their crucifixion, because clearly, you've met Christ Jesus himself. Move on.

Friends who walk in alignment with the Word of God can understand how we might, for example, begin losing faith after being unemployed or single for a long period of time. They will know how to

then encourage us to continue trusting Him. Among friends who make the walk, we can trust that recreational activities will promote Godliness, as opposed to a worldliness that would only move us further away from, rather than closer to God.

In seeking this most prized of relationships, we have to distinguish between which relationships will help us grow and which might otherwise lure us further away from God.

It can be painful. But it will sure be worth it.

Minister Meech explains that restoring his own relationship with God included "creating boundaries" in his life and having [Christian] "brothers I could talk to."

Marcia Y. says that when she has doubts or questions about her faith, she talks about these with her priest or another parish member whom she has come to trust. She says that sometimes, she will be "in a conversation with them, and they are answering [the questions] I have in my heart without me asking." High five, Holy Spirit. High five.

On the flipside, Margaret M. says that she maintains her relationship with God by not allowing other people's doubts to infiltrate her heart. "I try to separate myself," she emphasizes.

This can be hard (contrary to what the title of this chapter recommends,) but separating from negative energies will oftentimes propel us into better company. It's like clearing your garden of the weeds one week, then returning the next week to find your plants finally flourishing.

There are many real people out there, who know and *accept* the Word, who can pray with you to help build and nurture the relationship you seek.

Journal Starters

Open your journal entry with a simple prayer for help in your walk. Be still and ask the Holy Spirit to reveal people in your life who can help you in your walk. Then pay attention. Sometimes it can be a friend or colleague, a class or bible study. Use your journal to note potential relationships. Here are a few prompts to get you started.

1. The person (s) who I know has/have a relationship and believes is...

2. The first thing I would probably ask him/her about their faith and relationship with the Lord is...

Seek Ye First the
Kingdom of God...

3.

Seek Christ.

" **S**eek" is described in the Merriam Webster online dictionary as "a verb that means to attempt to find (something)." Synonyms include to search for, and to be on the lookout for.

A scavenger hunt is a game that gives contestants a list of items they must find within a certain location, within a certain time frame. In order to be successful at it, the winning contestant must find all items on the list before the other contestants do. It can be a fun, but extremely challenging exercise for many reasons. Maybe the location is a small space and there are many players. One must be quick in finding the objects or they will miss the opportunity. More important than moving quickly though, players must be familiar with items on the list in order to take possession of them and present them to the judges.

Let's say that there is a globe on that list. If you know what a globe is, and that they come in many different sizes and colors, the odds of winning are increased exponentially. If you've never seen one before however, you won't know that, and you will miss the opportunity to successfully identify it and win the game.

What if I told you that if you do not know who God is, it will be more difficult for you to be on the lookout for him?

What if I told you that if you do not know how the Devil operates, it will be easier for him to find you, steal from you, and destroy you?

Then, what if I told you that by seeking Christ *through His Word*, you will be able to identify Christ and Christ-like things at an amazing speed, no matter how big or small the place is that you're in? And that you will be able to better sidestep the Devil's traps because you'll be able to identify the tactics that he employs?

What if I told you that you will be able to identify miracles? And that your prayers can be powerful enough to bring them about?

You may not believe me right away, but I can prove it. The things I've been telling you in this book can also be found in the ultimate guide book, the greatest source of truths that no man can fully understand: the Bible.

The Bible reveals:

- **Who God is:** (the Great I am, Wonderful Counselor, the sure foundation, Yahweh, Emmanuel (God with us), the Prince of Peace, the Lion of Judah, The Beginning and the End – Alpha and Omega, and more;
- **God's great love for us:** He sacrificed His Son.
- **God's promises for our lives:**
  - to help us to prosper and not to harm us, to give us hope and a future (Jeremiah 29:11),
  - peace, when we are tired and broken (Matthew 11:18).
  - transformation from our former selves (2 Corinthians 3:18)
- **Every single thing we will ever want to know about how to get through this life.**

Don't believe me? Here's a short list.

How to love like Christ	*The Gospels and Letters*
What love really is	*1 Corinthians13:1-13*
How to pray	*The Book of Psalms*
How to manage money/ behave/ choose friends/ raise children/ succeed	*Proverbs, Ecclesiastes*
The fruits of the Spirit ("Good" or "Approved" attributes.) The fruit of the flesh (Sin.)	*Galatians 5*
What to say to romance your spouse	*Song of Songs*

When you are armed with the Word of God, you are well prepared for life. What do I mean by "prepared?" The dictionary says it means to have gotten ready beforehand. Therefore, reading your Bible is the way in which to prepare for what is to come.

"Being prepared" means that you will know the truth of Christ's teachings.

Christ's two main commandments are simple.

> *"Love the Lord your God with all your heart and with all your soul and with all your mind. This is the first and greatest commandment, And the second is like it: Love your neighbor as yourself." (Matthew 22:37-40)*

Christ names these as the most important rules not only to confound the lawyers who tested Him, but also because they encapsulate everything. If you love God, you will want to do everything to please Him; to be obedient, and to repent of your sins. If you love your neighbor you will treat him well, encourage him, console him, help him advance and protect him from harm.

But it doesn't stop there.

Reading the Bible helps us to better understand what Jesus' personality was like – loving, kind, understanding, inspiring, motivational, comforting, insightful (yes, He had a little help here), compassionate, and steadfast. I could just be selfish and fill the page with his attributes, but then you wouldn't be able to add any attributes for yourself. ☺. He teaches us love, obedience and sacrifice.

Reading the Bible helps us to understand His sacrifice. Jesus didn't want to die (Luke 22:42), but He did so because it was His Father's will, so that we would have forgiveness and receive eternal life.

Reading the Bible helps us remain in tune with whether or not what is being preached is in alignment with the Word of God. Many people have found themselves lost, in religious cults, because the Word was twisted by the proverbial wolf in sheep's clothing to convince them to worship a certain person or ideology that was not of God. If a wolf tells you something contradictory to what the Bible says Christ has said or done, you can be certain that this church or its servant (minister, deacon, or whomever) is not in alignment with Christ and you, should you choose to follow them, won't be either.

If you are not familiar with the Word, a study Bible is a good place to start. This will help you to get a better understanding because it includes easily understood notes and references. You can even subscribe to a feed or e-mail mailing list from your favorite pastors or Christian authors who can send you a devotional on a daily basis. Some are simple. Some are a little lengthy. But all will get you accustomed to seeing and reading God's word regularly. (YouVersion's Bible App is a great source.)

Prepared means you are well-versed in the tactics of the enemy – so you know when he's setting a trap.

When we see a mouse in the house, we have two options: to run from it or catch it. If we decide to catch it, there are some things we should know about mice in order to set a trap. We know they (proverbially) like cheese, so when we set a mousetrap, we put cheese on it. When the mouse leans forward for a nibble: *GOTCHA!*

That's how Satan works. We see it in the book of Matthew when Jesus had just finished his forty days and nights in the desert, and was weak, tired and hungry. (This is typically when the Devil gets into our own lives, too.) The Devil appeared (Matthew 4:3-11) and tested His power, His faith and His loyalty, to which Jesus responded "Get behind me Satan." When we know how the enemy works, we are better prepared to disengage his traps or to sidestep him.

When we know the Truth, it is easier to identify the voice of the Lord and to decipher and refute the lies of the enemy. When we can do that, we are drawn closer to God.

When we draw closer to Him, we are able to more easily put Him first in our lives.

Tyrone A. says that in order to keep God first, he had to recognize that "all that I have, I know who gave it to me. Everybody doesn't have it, and that those that do don't keep it. I put Him first because I realize where it came from."

> "But seek first his kingdom and his righteousness, and all these things will be given to you as well." (Matthew 6:33)

Nicole M. says, meanwhile, "I make sure I wake up thanking Him. I make sure to focus all my thoughts on Him."

> Psalm 5:3 says, "In the morning, LORD, you hear my voice; in the morning I lay my requests before you and wait expectantly."

Naomi L. reveals that she puts God first by acting as if He is a person; a friend. When she wants to do something, she'll simply say, "I want to do this. What do you think?" By keeping it light, "in a sense it makes it so easy." It puts "Him in a position where he is primary. If you involve Him, you'll never go wrong."

By treating God as a friend, allowing Him to clarify what is acceptable or not, we show him that we believe in Him, which makes us a friend in God's eyes.

> James 2:23 says, *"Abraham believed God, and it was credited to Him as righteousness, and he was called God's friend."*

Although each person has a different method of putting God first, each is in alignment with the Bible. When we don't know the Word, we get pigeonholed into doing things we may not understand, rendering the actions purposeless. But, if we do indeed know the Word, we soon find out that there are many routes to moving closer to God, because we have the guidebook to clarify.

Journal Starters

Open your journal entry with a simple prayer for understanding. Choose a scripture about Jesus that you are familiar with. Ask the Holy Spirit to guide you. Record your understanding of the verse.

List the time of day you can dedicate to meditating on the Word. Then go for it!

Tip: Keep it simple!

A good place to start putting God first is in the morning! Start your day with three words: Thank You Lord. It is thanksgiving. It is praise. It is exaltation. It is God at the start of your day.

One Step At A Time...

4.

Start slowly.

R enewing any relationship starts with taking the first step. Then another and another.

Nisla E., a dance educator, says that she feels closest to God when she goes to Him about small things. "[Those small things] remind me He's really here every step." And she means that both literally and figuratively. God's presence is a key factor for choreography inspiration—and much more. *"He's not only there when I have a good performance; He's there when I am practicing for that performance. He's there when I get up in the morning and am getting*

*ready to go to practice. It's seeing him in the
little stuff that makes me more intimate with
him."*

Check Yourself...

In a mature friendship, if we are feeling a little
distance between ourselves and the other person, we
might ask ourselves, did I do something to cause
this? Was I the one who started the fight? Did I give
him a reason to feel angry or disappointed? Was
that thing that I wanted, despite my friend's
annoyance with me or refusal to oblige, really worth
losing the relationship altogether? In the same way,
we might ask ourselves the same questions relating
to any distance we may feel from God.

With friends, this is often difficult to do. But
the answer could be that, no, it wasn't your fault at
all; your friend was the offending party. Or, it may
be that each of you could have played a part in the
estrangement. With God, however, any distance is
most definitely brought on by you.

He initiated the relationship and He seeks us.
But the depth of the relationship we have with God
is a direct result of the time and effort we put into it.
It's the difference between Him being simply an
acquaintance or a friend, and truly being our BFF:
Best friend forever.

Out on a Limb

The next step toward repairing a damaged friendship might be to call your friend. In the same way, we can also call on God. Pray to Him. Say hello. Ask for help. Say thank you. It may not seem like much, but it doesn't have to be extravagant.

Date Nights

Your next step, in repairing a friendship, might be to meet your friend for lunch. In the same way, you might set aside some time to talk to God: a longer conversation, maybe reading a Bible scripture. Next thing you know, you're shouting Him out on your way to work in the morning; studying a book of the Bible; attending church more frequently. It's like any friendship that has hit a snag. You know you love the person and really do want him around. In the case of God, it's guaranteed that our love will be returned because, as you will come to understand as you mature in Him, the love from God has never truly left you. It never will.

Reminders

Enid E. says that the times she feels furthest from God are after a victory. "It's like you're praying for something and, like the day after, you find it hard to pray. It's like pride says, YOU *did that instead of [acknowledging] GOD doing it. When I feel the emptiness, I go to Psalms 42, which says, 'As the deer pants for streams of water, so my soul pants for You, O God'."*

Sometimes, though this may seem strange, we may have to remind ourselves about God and His existence. If we've endured a season of lack, or even one of pain, it's easy to continue praying to and remembering God, because the victory has yet to arrive.

Let's go deeper.

How many of you women have prayed to God for a mate; said, "God, I am so lonely. If you send my husband, I will be so grateful. I will even name my first child after a holy prophet whose name I can't pronounce." You prayed and you prayed, and... Glory!

You got that mate but, well, you forgot to continue talking to God. Your praise waned. Your ministry went dry. Little Belthezzar made a safe entry into the world, but you let up on your promise to teach him the Word.

How many of you men have pursued a woman, courted her, treated her like royalty. But when she actually became your Queen, you forgot to make sure her crown stayed shiny, to continue buying flowers, to plan dates or just call her during the day to say hello. Basically, you stopped doing all you had done before to win her because, well, you already got the prize.

That woman? That man? That's how we often behave toward God, once we've gotten what we wanted. Our world becomes centered on that thing, that person. Either we totally disregard the thing (or person), or we may even disregard the Giver of that thing, Himself.

The most beautiful part of our relationship with God is that fortunately, He doesn't just wait around for us to seek Him. He also seeks us.

Minister Cee says that oftentimes "it is God that chases me; not the other way around."

Tyrone A. says that he noticed during a tour in the military that, although he was on a path opposing God, God "kept presenting himself and presenting opportunities" for Tyrone to turn to Him. Additionally, when Tyrone asked God to help Him stop smoking cigarettes, God gave him the strength to quit which, in turn, inspired him to trust and ask again and again, strengthening the relationship and drawing him closer.

God is our Father. He knows who we are. But we have to want the relationship with Him. We have to want it to grow. We have to remember Him in our daily lives. It starts with day one.

Journal Starters

Open your journal entry with a simple prayer for renewal of your relationship. Use your journal to write a letter to God. Remind Him of who you are and why you're seeking to renew this relationship; the real reason(s), not what you think sounds good to Him. Here are a few prompts to get you started.

1. Hey God? It's me [your name here]. (Then let it flow. He wants to hear it.)

2. Today, I need help with _____ to move closer to You, Lord. (Only list one thing. However, you can do this daily. Also, it's okay to repeat the same thing, but trying something new keeps it from becoming stale.)

We Fall Down But We Get Up...

5.

Do not expect perfection.

A person who wishes to become a welder must do an apprenticeship before he or she can be certified to work as and call him or herself a welder. It takes five years to move from apprenticeship—where a soon-to-be-welder learns the tricks of the trade—to becoming a journeyman. While learning, he or she is given the proper tools to work with and protect him or herself. Even with the right training and tools, the person will often endure burns and scars while acquiring experience. The same process applies to becoming a better disciple of Christ.

Children have to be corrected pretty often! Why? Because they are still learning the ins and outs of life. Fortunately, after a while, there are some things you won't have to tell them not to do anymore.

We Christians are all sinners, striving to do better. We are going to mess up. We are going to backslide. We are going to get angry. We are going to come again to a circumstance we thought we'd overcome, only to find that we still have work to do. This happens to everyone. But it's a process.

> *Malaika M. says "I remind myself I'm human and I'm going to make mistakes. But I try not to make that mistake again. I have to ask my flesh to die."*

> > *Galatians 5:16 says, "So I say, walk by the Spirit, and you will not gratify the desires of the flesh. For the flesh desires what is contrary to the Spirit and the Spirit contrary to the flesh."*

Sin comes from our natural inclination to prioritize satisfying the flesh rather than the Spirit.

> *Tyrone A. says, "Once I own it, and say 'I did that, I own it,' I say, 'let me not do that again. God's grace is sufficient so I can release it and allow God's warning signals to keep me on the right path."*

> > *1 Corinthians 10:13 says, "No temptation has overtaken you except what is common to*

mankind. And God is faithful; he will not let you be tempted beyond what you can bear. But when you are tempted, he will also provide a way out so that you can endure it."

God knows we will be tempted on this journey but, somehow, He always offers a detour to reroute us from a treacherous path.

Naomi L. believes that when you go off track, "You have to engage God. The enemy encourages you to run away from Him. The Word does not convict you."

Proverbs 18:10 says, "The name of the LORD is a fortified tower; the righteous run to it and are safe."

David runs to God in times of turmoil; the times when he has allowed his flesh to rule him. He knows he's flawed, but he trusts God to help him.

He says in Psalm 51:10-12, "Create in me a pure heart, O God, and renew a steadfast spirit within me. Do not cast me from your presence or take your Holy Spirit from me. Restore to me the joy of your salvation and grant me a willing spirit, to sustain me."

Understanding that God is there for us when we sin is like a soothing ointment on bruised skin.

When we repent and surrender, God works in us and through us until, after a while, He won't have to keep telling us what to do and what not to do, in regards to sin. Eventually, we will just no longer have a taste for these sins. (That's called deliverance. Praise God.) And even then, there will be things we have to battle against. We will have to call on God to help us and to forgive us for the rest of our lives. We must KEEP CALM – and call on God.

Journal Starters

Open your journal entry with a simple prayer request of revelation. Be still and ask the Holy Spirit to reveal the areas where you often experience weakness and a tendency to revert to the old you. Use your journal to record your thoughts. Here are a few prompts to get you started.

1. The time(s) when I seem to revert back to the old me is when…

2. The times I feel weakest are when…

And then pray to the Father for help in overcoming or removing the circumstances or people who lead you back "there."

Be transparent with God.

6

Talk to Him about your fears, concerns, desires, and disappointments.

God already knows us. He made us.

Psalm 139:13 says, "For you created my inmost being; you knit me together in my mother's womb. I praise you because I am fearfully and wonderfully made; your works are wonderful, I know that full well. My frame was not hidden from you when I was made in the secret place."

God was there when and where your mother and father made you. And there aren't many places more private than that. Before your parents even met; before they even got to that place, He knew you. Who you were, who you would become, where you would fall and how you would rise, even whether or not you would fall again after that. He knew and knows it all. It just takes a while for us to be able to say those not so good things (that He already knows about us) to Him. When we finally do say them out loud, we do so displaying a trust in Him.

> *Marcia Y. says, "I hold nothing back. I think He sees everything and knows what's in our hearts."*

David goes to God for everything, always acknowledging that He is sovereign and omniscient - knowing all things about us. It only makes sense to reveal our hurts, wants, shortcomings, mistakes, disappointments, desires to God.

When we do that, we acknowledge those fears, concerns, desires, and even those disappointments, as well as how they hurt us or hold us back. When we open up to do that, we open ourselves to another side of Him: God as revealer.

Revelation is God's thing. He revealed things to Moses. He revealed things to Aaron. He revealed things to Noah. He revealed things to David. He revealed the most Wondrous of all things to Mary.

All of these people had legitimate fears and concerns that they might have been cautious about admitting to God.

Imagine you're Moses in the desert and God shows up as a burning bush.

First thought: That bush is weird. Second thought: And why is its flame not burning out? Third thought, while casually inching away: Is it really talking, or am I tripping? Nope, you determine, the bush called my name. It's God.

So then you ask Him how to answer the many questions of the Israelites. He tells you the words to say, and even shows you miracles to perform! Yet, even still, your heart is filled with worry and doubt.

Moses (to himself): Dang. I stutter. But I don't really want to tell God that I'm nervous about being His go-to-guy right now. *sigh.* Let me gently remind him that I stutter.

Moses (to God): Hey, um, excuse me, God? I…just thought I should remind you…I have a stuttering problem.

According to the author: God rolls his eyes and continues to check His e-mail.

God (Exodus 3:11, as interpreted by the author): I know you stutter, Moses. I made you!

Moses: But God, please find someone else. Please.

According to the author: God closes His email and looks over his reading glasses.

God (Exodus 3:14 as interpreted by the author): Don't make me smite you out here today Moses Aloysius Smith. Fine. Your brother will help you.

Simple.

Moses confided in God. God helped him. So when we talk to Him about our own challenges, He will encourage us and/or send us help, too.

Maturing in Christ

Being transparent also means being receptive to tackling the most difficult areas of our lives: our own development.

Ask Him to show you where you need the help. Or correction. Ask Him to show you what's hindering you from moving into a new season in your life.

For years, I worked in a job I did not like. I would draft a resignation letter every month, or so it seemed, but I never would hand it in. I applied for other jobs. Nothing. God, why? I wondered. One day, Dr. Bernard preached a word on excellence – that it meant doing the small things properly, so that the larger elements, in the end, worked properly. Small things done well. It touched my heart. All this time I thought grandiose was the hallmark of excellence. But grandiose often proved too difficult to achieve and lacked substance.

Around the same time, He brought a person into my life who relied on shortcuts and minimal effort as his means to acquire the things he desired in life. I despised it in him. It reeked of mediocrity. And one day it clicked, though, that I also do that, too, sometimes. I had not realized I had been living with mediocrity as my standard, and that I wouldn't move into a new season until I trusted God to retrain me and to then, exercise and expect excellence from myself. It changed my life.

It's hard to open up like that. Because when you do, God will move in your life. Our comfort zones will be disrupted and the things we were accustomed to doing before become things that God disposes of, if he has no use for them.

It is necessary in order to draw closer to Him. But when you do, you'll be surprised to see how He will prepare you for the future he has in store for you.

Maybe you don't know what to say or what to ask for. That's okay. Just be truthful.

Ask for forgiveness. Tell Him what caused you to stray away. Tell Him about your disappointments, and how they made you feel. Sometimes you will actually get to see some of the very things He was saving you from or preparing you for. While other times, you will just never know why something didn't turn out the way you planned. But you can rest assured that, whatever it was, it was not to your detriment: God does nothing to harm us (Jeremiah 29:11.)

Opening up to God, crying out to Him, choosing to lay our hearts bare... these things open our hearts to receive healing and understanding via the Holy Spirit, through which we gain maturity and wisdom. Once we have wisdom, we are on our way to the fullness of life that God desires for us.

Journal Starters

Open your journal entry with a prayer for transparency. Be still and ask the Holy Spirit to open your heart. Use your journal as a starting point to close the gap in your relationship. Or maybe you want to talk to Him about this one particular thing. There is no right or wrong answer, experience, or feeling. Here are a few prompts to get you started.

1. The one thing that I've kept tucked away from Jesus is the time when...

2. The other thing that I've kept "hidden" from Jesus is...

Go to him in prayer about it. Apologize if you need to. Cry if you need to. Let it out. It's not a surprise to Him, but it frees you, I promise.

Fall On Your Knees...

7.

Pray.

Prayer, in my best summation, is an act of communicating with God. At the start of every journal entry, we started with prayer. This was intentional. Although it is listed as the seventh way to renew your relationship with Christ, it is, and always will be the most important part of your relationship. Without prayer, there is no communication, so the distance widens.

Now, some prayers, such as the Lord's Prayer, are from biblical texts. But prayer, as we stated can also comprise a personal, one-on-one conversation with God; one which involves both talking to and listening to Him, as well.

All but one person interviewed for this book listed prayer as among their methods for renewing and maintaining relationship with God. (And I am 99.9% sure that was an oversight.) It's such a personal experience that we cannot help but draw closer to Him during these times.

Prayer can take on many forms.

It can be:

- An ongoing stream of consciousness: Hey God, it's me. Just wanted to say hey. And thanks for today. It was hard, but You kept me. Can You also keep the Knicks in the playoffs? And the neighbor's kids off my lawn? And mostly, can You help get my figure intact after this baby gets here? Please and thanks.

- A form of worship: God, You are awesome. I exalt You this day. I lift You up for praise God, not because of anything You did for me, but just because of who You are. That sunrise this morning? Magnificent. You are an awesome God. There is none greater and I thank You for allowing me to witness your greatness.

- A distress call: Mayday Lord! 9-1-1 Emergency! I need Your help!

- A form of thanksgiving: Thank You, Lord, for the health of my family. Thank You, God, for the financial miracle that has kept a roof overhead. Thank You, God, for feeding and clothing us.. Thank You, Sweet

Jesus, for loving me. Thank You for who You are.

- A time to help others: Lord, my neighbor is struggling with her son. Lord, I pray for Your grace over their home and that You grant her the strength and patience to endure. God, I donated money to my church sister's cancer treatment. But that's not enough. I need Your mercy and Your healing to wash over her.

Sometimes we get caught up in thinking our prayers have to be formal and stiff. Spoken in an English accent and in the King James vernacular:

Dearest Father that doth ruleth all the Eartheth. Thou dost not understandeth me for I dost not understandeth myself either. (pronounced eye-ther, not ee-ther.)

Ummm, no.

I mean, it's fine if you feel comfortable with it, but saying the words like that does not make your prayer any more official in God's eyes. What matters is your surrender, the sincerity of your heart, your faith when you're asking and your genuine desire for the relationship. That's when we really get to experience God in our lives. That's when we really witness His miraculous hand. That's when He truly begins to reveal Himself to us.

Sometimes we don't know what to say, but all we have to do is say what's on our minds, in our hearts. It's not that He doesn't already know; God's like a best friend who you just trust with your innermost secrets, but better. He'll never repeat them!

Pray with praise in your heart, giving thanks for His presence. Pray for His everlasting peace. Pray for wisdom and understanding. Pray with the purpose of worship and in acknowledgment of His grace, mercy, and unfailing love.

A relationship is a two-way street. We cannot expect to only lift our hands to receive. We have to also give. God is all-knowing, all merciful and all-everything awesome. But we need to be mindful that the relationship is not based solely on our own wants; that it is also based on sincere love and adoration that we have for Him; the same that He has for us.

I pray you give your heart (back) to the Lord today.

If you have never given your life to Christ; or have already been born again, but have turned away and want to step back into His loving arms, all you have to say is:

"Father, I dedicate my life to You today. I confess and repent of my sins. I thank You for the sacrifice of Your Son, Jesus Christ, who died on the cross and rose again so that I could be washed clean in His blood, forgiven, and born again. Thank You for taking me back. In Jesus name. Amen."

And it is so.

Journal Starters

Open your journal entry with a prayer of magnification and praise! Be still and ask the Holy Spirit to guide you in prayer. Use your journal to make a list of what you will pray for. Here are a few prompts to get you started.

1. God, You are awesome because…

2. God, I thank You for…

3. God, forgive me for…

4. God, I pray on behalf of…

5. God, please help me with…

My prayer for you is that you continue to seek His face daily so that you can develop the deepest and most fulfilling relationship of your life. He's got great plans for you.

Prayer Resources

YouVersion App (Available on iPhone and Android)
- Full Bible in many versions: AMP, CEB, ESV, KJV, MSG, NIV, NKJV, NLT, etc.
- Access to friends and other users
- Access to devotionals (3 days, 7 days, month-long, year-long; for women, for singles, for married couples, for business, etc.)

Girlfriends Pray Prayer Line
Monday to Friday 7am and 10pm,
+ 12 noon on Wednesdays
712-775-7031 PIN 943334#

Manhood Legacy Prayer Line
Monday to Friday @ 7am
712-432-3082 PIN 506450

www.ingramcontent.com/pod-product-compliance
Lightning Source LLC
Chambersburg PA
CBHW031629040426
42452CB00007B/739